CREATING PORTFOLIOS

For Success in School, Work, and Life

MARTIN KIMELDORF

EDITED BY PAMELA ESPELAND

free spirit
PUBLISHING®

Works
for kids™

Dedicated to the one who lives in my soul's portfolio,
Judy K.

Acknowledgments

I wish to acknowledge the following people for providing essential editorial assistance, creative criticism, contributions, and support during the development of this book about portfolios:

- ✪ Timberline High School teachers Pam Mortillaro, Kristin Miller, and Chad Kerrihard.

- ✪ River Ridge High School teacher Sharon Moorehead and her class.

- ✪ Recognized portfolio experts Judith Arter, Northwest Regional Education Laboratory, and Jane Sanborn, Far West Laboratory for Educational Research and Development.

- ✪ Judy Galbraith at Free Spirit Publishing for taking another publishing adventure with me. She quickly committed the needed resources to bring this book out in the shortest possible time, thereby supplying teachers and students with the tools they need.

- ✪ Pamela Espeland, who graced this book with her excellent editing insights. In the process, we have gone from editor-writer to friends, and a new friend like her makes writing all the more worthwhile.

CONTENTS

LIST OF REPRODUCIBLE PAGES

Introduction

My father's work area was tucked into a well-lit corner in the back of the garage. Spread out across his workbench were dozens of jars and small boxes filled with various light sockets, bolts, fasteners and tacks, washers, electrical connectors, rubber gadgets, and plastic whatchamacallits. He was a lifelong collector and organizer of stuff. Besides hardware, he also collected photos, rocks, plants, recipes, articles, cartoons, and quotes from famous people. And, as I was growing up, my father stuffed a large envelope with the memorabilia that marked the different stages in my life.

This envelope grew fat with my first job card for being a milk monitor, photos of my first magic show, report cards from elementary through high school, an athletic letter for tennis, letters I wrote once I left home, articles about civil rights marches I attended, poems published in a school newspaper, drawings, maps of a 150-mile bike trip I took with my brother, and so on. Fortunately, before my father died, he organized most of the items in photo albums and scrapbooks. Later, in my journals, I wrote about the memories he collected and stored for us. Today, I love to go back and look through all the stuff.

I have followed in my father's footsteps because I, too, became a collector. And, as a result, I have enjoyed keeping journals and making scrapbooks. Perhaps because my father and I collected so many things, I found it easier than most people to write a résumé describing my talents. Likewise, I had all the information I needed for applications to jobs and colleges. Organizing my "workbench" came naturally to me.

In this book, you'll learn how you can create a portfolio that illustrates your proud moments. If you've ever kept a journal, made a scrapbook, or kept track of your life in a photo album, you'll find that creating a portfolio is very similar. A portfolio is simply a collection of samples. Your portfolio can tell a story, demonstrate your interests, talents, contributions, and studies, and show off your finest efforts for others to see.

About This Book

Creating Portfolios begins by describing four types of portfolios. Each type may have a different purpose and a different audience.

Some portfolios are done for school or for individual teachers. Yours might contain samples that represent your learning in a particular class or over a given period of time. Some instructors will tell you exactly what to include in your portfolio, while others will give you a lot of freedom. For instance, you might be asked to include a sample of a rough draft and your best writing, your best test score, evidence of research, examples of critical thinking, and an exhibit illustrating teamwork. Or you might simply be told to collect examples of your most important experiences and explain how each one demonstrates a skill or special knowledge. This latter type of portfolio is wide-open and may be an essential part of a culminating class project or be required for graduation from junior high, high school, or college. You might be asked to create a portfolio somewhere between these two extremes, where some items are required and you can decide what else to include.

Another type of portfolio illustrates talents or skills you have mastered which might be of interest to an employer, college admissions person, or bank loan officer. For instance, if you wanted money to set up a computer art class for the summer, your portfolio could include samples of your art work, teaching skills, and business knowledge. You would show your portfolio to a banker when applying for a loan.

Some people create portfolios for themselves. Yours could be a collection of photos, letters, and stories about your favorite people—the ones you might not see again after you move or graduate. This type of portfolio may become very important to you many years from now.

In other words, portfolios can come in all shapes and sizes. By thinking broadly about portfolios, you'll come to realize that yours can include many different kinds of samples: computer printouts, blueprints, recipes, photos, and award certificates; actual objects such as videos, plaques, jewelry, athletic pins, or letters; certificates from a knowledge bowl; even letters of thanks from people you have helped.

After introducing the four basic types of portfolios, this book describes the three steps involved in building a portfolio. Just follow the directions and do the exercises. Background information and examples will help you know exactly what to do.

❖ *In Step One, you consider the question, "What samples should I begin collecting for my portfolio?"*

Exercises help you to recall and brainstorm experiences important in your life. These moments of personal pride and joy begin to suggest who you are and what you are good at and enjoy doing. You start to identify samples that tell the story of your learning and living. As you reflect about your experiences and gather items from across a span of time, you'll find that you have collected ten or more samples before you know it. These items make up your "working portfolio."

⚙ *In Step Two, you select and organize items from your working portfolio which best tell your portfolio story.*

This step begins with the question, "Who is going to see my portfolio?" In other words, "Who is my audience?" Your audience might include teachers, parents, employers, friends, college personnel, review boards, coaches, or customers. Once you think about your audience and what they are looking for, you will have a better sense of which samples to select for your portfolio.

Next, you need to organize or sequence your samples. You start by looking for connections between them. For instance, you might put them in chronological order, group them according to the skills they represent, or group them by themes representing the experiences in your life.

Once your samples are organized, you develop a description for each sample or group that tells your audience why a particular item is important in your portfolio. You might describe the skills or talents you used, the obstacles you overcame, and how the experience benefited you personally.

You complete your portfolio by creating the front matter—a cover or title page, table of contents, introduction, and acknowledgments. (Did you read the front matter in this book?) You might also create back matter to conclude or sum up your work.

⚙ *In Step Three, you prepare for an oral presentation of your portfolio.*

More and more schools and colleges are asking students to share their portfolios with a review panel of peers, staff, or community representatives. This is much easier than you might think. By the time you reach this step, you have already done the planning, thinking, and creating. The third step is simply a review of the samples contained in your portfolio.

Your Portfolio and Your Future

Are adults always asking you, "What do you want to be when you grow up"? That's a tough question. It requires you to project into the future and identify your goals. It means taking a risk and setting a direction for your life.

Before you can make a choice about the future, you must look over your past and evaluate the most important events, experiences, and decisions in your life. This is exactly why a portfolio is important. It helps you to inventory who you are, what you enjoy, and what you do best. The story told in your portfolio summarizes where you've been, and this helps you to determine where you want to go next. Your portfolio can help you to choose future pathways.

Mastering the process of self-evaluation and goal-setting is essential for success in the next century, when most people will likely change jobs and careers many times. Each time you change jobs or go back for more training, you'll ask yourself, "What do I want to be, what do I enjoy doing, what am I good at?" Many working adults today are asking themselves, "What do I want to become *next*?" When you ask yourself that question, you'll find part of the answer in your portfolio.

This book invites you to prepare for success in the future by creating a portfolio today. When you're finished, your portfolio will present the most important story you have to tell: *your* story. I know you'll feel very proud when it is completed.

PORTFOLIOS: A DEFINITION

A portfolio is a collection of samples that communicate your interests and give evidence of your talents. You use your portfolio to show others what you have accomplished, learned, or produced.

You can think of your portfolio as a special-purpose autobiography. How useful and important it is to you depends on what you put into it.

There is no one "right" way to build a portfolio. In the past, most portfolios came in binders, leather carrying cases, or scrapbooks. They might have been accompanied by boxes to hold objects. Today you might include computer disks, multimedia CD-ROMs, videos, and audio recordings.

Four Types of Portfolios

There are many types of portfolios. This book shows you how to create four of the most useful types. Your final product will depend on the requirements of your school, potential customers, or employers. Or you might decide to create a portfolio for your own pleasure and interest.

If you've ever enjoyed making and later looking at photo albums, slide shows, or homemade videos, then you'll enjoy the experience of creating a portfolio and sharing it with others. You can include just about anything— essays you've written, quotes from others, brochures, maps, photos, drawings, songs, poetry, computer disks, video tapes, music tapes, jewelry, dried leaves, science lab slides, displays, samples of different types of woods, fabrics, and so on. What you include depends on what you want to show about yourself.

Student Portfolio

Increasingly, teachers and schools are requiring student portfolios in class and graduation requirements because they can show more about your accomplishments and learning than a simple multiple-choice test or semester grade.

The primary purpose of a student portfolio is to demonstrate what you have learned in a given class or across a certain part of your school career. Your portfolio might include samples of a process or procedure you have mastered, an effort you have made, or specific knowledge or skills you have acquired.

⚙ Your math teacher might require you to include samples of using different mathematical tools (calculators, computers, compass), applications of measuring skills, experiences where math was used in other classes, and examples of how you have used math to collect, analyze, and display data.

- Your English teacher could ask you to include sample dialogues from plays you have read and enjoyed, a formal letter, an essay arguing a point of view, a book review, a personal newsletter describing your life, and a journal entry.

- Your art teacher could ask for samples of your beginning and final drawings to show growth, a color chart, photos of your best works, and descriptions of artists or art works you most enjoy.

While a student portfolio generally includes samples of your finest work, you may also be asked to show how you have improved. This means that you'll need to include both beginning samples of your art work, calligraphy, or rough draft essays and samples of your final, polished works.

More and more schools are offering integrated or block classes where students combine their learning from several different disciplines such as art, drama, and social studies. Your portfolio for these classes might be guided by the themes or projects in which all students participate.

- In a class called "Fine Arts and History," students studied a certain period of history, read a play about that period, and staged a play using lighting, props, and make-up. For their portfolios, students were asked to include examples of work which fit one of three themes: "The Drama of Human Conflict," "A Scenario for Cooperation," or "Cultural Images Reflecting Diversity."

Colleges are catching the portfolio fever. More and more college instructors are requiring their students to complete a portfolio as part of the class.

You may be asked to prepare a graduation portfolio to summarize what you have learned across your entire school career. This kind of portfolio could include letters of reference from teachers, school assignments you are proud of, athletic or club awards, examples of membership in different groups, projects you completed, and so on.

Student portfolios don't have to be limited to classroom experiences. You might also include examples of learning things on your own or using your skills outside of school. For instance, you might show how you used geometric principles to design a garden, how you applied communication skills on the job, and how you used ideas from course readings and discussions to better understand people who are different from you. Or you might be asked to include examples from home, school, and community experiences related to your accomplishments and interests in three areas: vocational preparation, leisure and personal wellness, and community service.

Sometimes teachers will use your student portfolio as part of their evaluation or grading of your work. Your final course grade might be based in part on what you learned and the skills you acquired, with your portfolio giving the evidence of your learning and accomplishments.

Project Portfolio

A project portfolio is like a documentary film showing the effort or sequence of steps that went into a project or independent study.

- Your portfolio for a power technology class might include pictures of different machines and materials used to produce a solar-powered car.

- Your portfolio for a music class might include sheet music, a record of your hours of practice, and an audiotape or videotape from your final performance.

- Your portfolio for a community service project might show how you developed an idea to put in a new bus shelter for residents of a nursing home. It could include the designs you developed, the city permits you completed, letters you wrote, bills for materials, photographs of the finished shelter, and the letter you received from the residents of the nursing home thanking you.

- Your portfolio for producing a school play might include the script, the research you did on the characters, and pictures of your make-up, costume, and stage set. It could also include a newspaper article reviewing the play. Later, you might want to apply for a grant to do another production. You could use your portfolio to demonstrate that, if you got the grant, you would do a good job. Or, if you wanted to be chosen to direct a play, you might be asked to prove that you know all aspects of putting on a play. Your portfolio would become your proof.

Expert and Professional Portfolios

In an expert portfolio, your goal or assignment is to pick a topic to become an expert in. Sometimes you'll pick a topic jointly with another expert, a mentor, or a teacher. Because you already have an interest in the subject, you probably have some background information about it. Your goal is to broaden and deepen your knowledge. You do this by reading books, magazines, and articles, talking with people, networking with local experts for advice, and searching electronic databases. Then you inventory and organize your information. Think of this portfolio as a cross between a research paper and a scavenger hunt.

- To become an expert wood carver, I read wood carving magazines, took an evening course, studied types of woods, collected designs, gathered samples of wood stains and finishes, took photos of my early carvings, and created model or study boards (where sample carvings techniques are tried out and perfected). I kept notes or journal entries about various wood carvers and their techniques. Finally, I organized this scrapbook into a formal portfolio which I now use as a reference. I return to carving about every five years and add new ideas and samples. As a result, my portfolio has become a collection of my expertise, and it is invaluable in my pursuit of wood carving.

Once you combine expertise with experience in a given field, you are ready to create a professional portfolio. You might use it to look for a job or customers who would be interested in hiring you as a professional.

- Suppose you have just graduated from a business program, and you want to work as an executive secretary or administrative assistant. Instead of just showing up at the job interview with a résumé, you could come with a portfolio showing several ways you have used office technology and techniques. Your portfolio might include different posters done with computer graphics software, spreadsheets and charts done in spreadsheet applications, a multimedia presentation on disk, or a newsletter you designed with a desktop publishing program. You could also include samples of office memos, letters to customers, and videos showing how you handle customer service calls.

- Or you might want to start your own landscaping business. You could arrive at a customer's house with a portfolio full of pictures showing different gardens you have worked on or designed. It could include samples of the plants and shrubs that grow best in your area, along with a price list. You might also add awards you earned in a bonsai tree show, blue ribbons from a home and garden show, and letters from satisfied customers you received while working for someone else.

- One pair of high school students completed an award-winning portfolio for their child care class. It contained a statement of their philosophy about child care, blueprints for setting up their own child care setting, a budget, list of local resources, statements of policy regarding discipline and customers, and a large number of lessons, all neatly organized and presented in a binder. The students decided to go into business for themselves, so they added some planning steps for setting up a business. Then they renamed their binder "Child Care Business Plan and Portfolio." They made an appointment with a bank loan officer and eventually walked away with a start-up loan for their new business.

- Teachers applying for jobs are discovering that they can use portfolios when interviewing with principals and committees. A teacher's portfolio might include lesson plans, letters from students and parents, pictures of exciting moments in class, pictures of bulletin boards, newspaper stories about a class or school, grades from professors, a statement of one's teaching philosophy, a list of conferences and specialized training attended, and a résumé.

Professional portfolios need to be well designed, carefully planned, and presented in an organized and artistic way. You are showing a customer or employer why you think you are the best person for the job. You are proving your claims of talents using pictures, words, and perhaps objects.

Personal Portfolio

Unlike other types of portfolios, this one is done just for you. It's like a scrapbook of things that interest you.

✿ As a painter, you might like to collect photographs of your favorite paintings and other works that inspire you, and paint chips that show you which colors to mix. You might also include writings by artists in the form of notes or quotes, techniques recorded with the camera or in words, and personal journal entries summarizing your thoughts about your artwork.

✿ Perhaps you're a graduating senior and you want to create a "yearbook" type of portfolio. You could use desktop publishing to design different pages featuring your favorite people, subjects, projects, events, and places. You might include writings about the people and experiences that shaped your personality, results from a career interest and leisure test, brochures or applications from colleges you want to attend and jobs you want to get after graduation, even pictures from your family album to show how you have changed. Your final portfolio helps you to take stock of who you are and may indicate where you're going next.

SHARING YOUR PORTFOLIO WITH THE WORLD

Have you heard the words *e-mail, virtual reality, virtual community,* and *Internet?* They describe an emerging technology where people communicate with one another over computer networks. By connecting your phone line or TV cable to your computer, you can send mail electronically (e-mail), post messages on electronic bulletin board services (BBSs), and chat with people halfway across the planet. Imagine what you can learn and who you might meet in "cyberspace"!

In their book, *Electronic Job Search Revolution* (John Wiley & Sons Inc., 1994), Joyce Lain Kennedy and Thomas J. Morrow describe future job hunters who begin their search for work by tapping into the online labor market. They look up employers and jobs online, post their resumes in a job bank library, and are interviewed by videophone or other computerized service.

When you start job-hunting in the not-too-distant future, you might find an online request for your portfolio. You'll design your electronic portfolio using words, pictures, video clips, and sounds, then transmit it to a prospective employer on CD-ROM or over the wires. In other words, you might describe your talents at arc welding or laboratory analysis, include short films demonstrating your abilities, add sounds, animation, titles, maybe even music, then send it all by modem to someone in another city or another country. In the future, you might receive requests for your portfolio from very distant places.

BRAINSTORMING ABOUT EXPERT, PERSONAL, AND PROJECT PORTFOLIOS

This exercise helps you think about who might create an expert, personal, or project portfolio.

Expert and Personal Portfolios

1. Consider the different kinds of people who might use a portfolio to demonstrate or record expertise they have acquired. Read the list and check *three* kinds of people who might benefit from making a portfolio. Pick people you would find interesting, or come up with your own ideas.

    ☐ An athlete who wants to join a special training camp

    ☐ A computer hacker who wants to join a new computer club

    ☐ A person who enjoys decorating and wants a job decorating homes

    ☐ A person who wants to raise money for a park cleanup community service project

    ☐ A student who has tutored and studied teaching and wants to be a summer camp counselor

    ☐ A singer who wants to join a choir

    ☐ A risk-taker who wants to join a mountain climbing team

    ☐ A student who is asked to demonstrate different welding skills in an apprentice program

    ☐ A person who wants to keep a record of the places he or she has visited

    ☐ A person who is moving to a different town and wants to leave with a portfolio of memories

    ☐ A person who will be hospitalized for a while and needs cheering up

    ☐ A person who is running for political office

    ☐ A young adult who wants to put on magic shows for money in the summer

    ☐ A person who is studying another language on his or her own

    ☐ A musician who wants to join a band

    ☐ A person who wants a job in a child care center

    ☐ A person who loves to cook and eat great food

    ☐ A person who enjoys playing different kinds of games

    ☐ A person who loves animals and wants to become a pet trainer

    ☐ A person who _____

☐ An ability you'd like to demonstrate: _____

☐ Something you'd like to become expert in: _____

2. For each person or idea you checked, list five things which might be included in a portfolio.

   a. Person or idea: _____

      ✿ _____

      ✿ _____

      ✿ _____

      ✿ _____

      ✿ _____

   b. Person or idea: _____

      ✿ _____

      ✿ _____

      ✿ _____

      ✿ _____

      ✿ _____

   c. Person or idea: _____

      ✿ _____

      ✿ _____

      ✿ _____

      ✿ _____

      ✿ _____

3. Brainstorm with others to come up with five more things which might be included in each portfolio.

   a. Person or idea: _____

      ✿ _____

      ✿ _____

      ✿ _____

      ✿ _____

      ✿ _____

   b. Person or idea: _____

      ✿ _____

      ✿ _____

      ✿ _____

      ✿ _____

      ✿ _____

c. Person or idea: _____

    ✿ _____

    ✿ _____

    ✿ _____

    ✿ _____

    ✿ _____

4. Imagine that you have been asked to turn in a list of five samples for your own personal portfolio. Your portfolio could be about a person, a hobby, a career, a certain type of music, foods you enjoy, or just about anything that interests you. It must have a positive subject, and it must demonstrate your interests and talents.

Decide on your topic, then describe your samples. Explain what each sample tells about you.

Topic: _____

a. Sample: _____

What it tells about me:_____

_____

_____

b. Sample: _____

What it tells about me:_____

_____

_____

c. Sample: _____

What it tells about me:_____

_____

_____

d. Sample: _____

What it tells about me:_____

_____

_____

e. Sample: _____

What it tells about me:_____

_____

_____

Project Portfolio Warm-Up Worksheet

A project portfolio records the various experiences or steps you completed in order to plan, develop, and finish a project. If you will be doing a project portfolio in the near future, you can start thinking now about what might go into it. Your ideas might change several times along the way, so you may want to make several copies of this Warm-Up Worksheet.

1. VISION: What do you hope to accomplish in this project? What will happen? What will you build, change, or learn?

    _____

    _____

    _____

    _____

    _____

2. STEPS: What activities will you do to complete your project? You don't have to list them in order.

    ○ _____
    ○ _____
    ○ _____
    ○ _____
    ○ _____
    ○ _____
    ○ _____
    ○ _____
    ○ _____
    ○ _____

3. SAMPLES: Look over your vision and steps. List five things you might gather samples of, take pictures of, or collect.

    ○ _____
    ○ _____
    ○ _____
    ○ _____
    ○ _____

BRAINSTORMING ABOUT STUDENT PORTFOLIOS

Suppose you're asked to complete a portfolio as part of a requirement for a course or graduation ceremony, an application for a scholarship or mini-grant proposal, or a self-evaluation (or grade) for a class. If this your situation, you'll need a list from the teacher, agency, or institution telling you which items or types of samples need to be included in your portfolio. Your portfolio might then be judged against the list of required samples.

Sometimes you'll get a general list of items, and at other times a very specific list. This exercise helps you to think about and plan the kinds of samples you might include.

General List

Your teachers might ask you to collect samples from general areas representing your academic and vocational pursuits, leisure interests, and volunteer and service activities. Deciding exactly what items to include in your portfolio is up to you.

✿　One teacher asked her "Home and Family Life" students to include samples of good communication, personal goal-setting, job-finding documents, family values, and personal values in their portfolios.

Assume that you are required to include one sample for each of the following areas. Describe your samples.

1. Your best work from your favorite class.

　　_____

　　_____

2. An occupation or career you might be interested in.

　　_____

　　_____

3. A personal challenge you met. *Examples:* passing a tough class; filling out several job applications perfectly; trying out for a team; trying out for something you've never done before, like a school play; changing your diet; changing a behavior; changing an attitude; getting along in a difficult situation; competing in a contest or competition.

　　_____

　　_____

4. A leisure interest.

　　_____

　　_____

5. A project you were proud of completing—something that took a long time to do and required persistence, organization, and problem-solving.

_____

_____

6. A time when you showed leadership. *Examples:* attending a conference; planning a meeting; assisting at a school function; organizing a fund-raiser, newsletter, or service project; recruiting speakers; running for office.

_____

_____

Specific List

Your teachers might tell you exactly what items or types of samples to include in your portfolio. You'll need to demonstrate that you can meet the criteria and expectations of a specific audience. Your portfolio may be judged against the list of required samples.

○ A science instructor required students to include a specific assignment from each of the major lab experiments.

○ An instructor in a computer-assisted drafting course asked for samples of charts, blueprints, and schematics. Students were also required to include a budget or list of materials for designs they completed.

○ Students in a health-aide training class were asked to include a CPR card, a brochure they made about aging, personal safety tests, an HIV training certificate, and a test showing their mastery of medical terminology .

If you have been assigned a portfolio that must include specific items, start by listing them. Then try to think of samples that appeal to you *and* meet the requirements. You might change your mind several times about what to include, so you may want to make several copies of the Specific List Worksheet on pages 16–17.

NOTE

Instead of being given a list, you might be asked to compile a portfolio demonstrating what you have learned both in school and outside of school during your learning career. If your task is this general, start with Exercise 4 on pages 23–29.

Specific List Worksheet

1. Required item: _____
   Ideas for samples:
   - ○ _____
   - ○ _____
   - ○ _____

2. Required item: _____
   Ideas for samples:
   - ○ _____
   - ○ _____
   - ○ _____

3. Required item: _____
   Ideas for samples:
   - ○ _____
   - ○ _____
   - ○ _____

4. Required item: _____
   Ideas for samples:
   - ○ _____
   - ○ _____
   - ○ _____

5. Required item: _____
   Ideas for samples:
   - ○ _____
   - ○ _____
   - ○ _____

6. Required item: _____
   Ideas for samples:
   - ○ _____
   - ○ _____
   - ○ _____

7. Required item: _____

   Ideas for samples:

   ○ _____

   ○ _____

   ○ _____

8. Required item: _____

   Ideas for samples:

   ○ _____

   ○ _____

   ○ _____

9. Required item: _____

   Ideas for samples:

   ○ _____

   ○ _____

   ○ _____

10. Required item: _____

   Ideas for samples:

   ○ _____

   ○ _____

   ○ _____

Creating Your Working Portfolio

You begin creating your working portfolio by thinking about yourself. You might ask yourself, "What can I collect and possibly include in a portfolio which is important to me? Which items am I proud of? Which ones show what I have accomplished? Which ones tell my story best?" Even if you are told to include specific types of things—such as a letter, test, photograph, or computer chart—you must still decide on the individual items.

The exercises in this section help you to start thinking about your experiences, interests, and talents, and the samples you might choose to represent them in your portfolio.

EXERCISE 3

WHAT COULD YOU PUT IN YOUR SHOE BOX?

Many people begin a working portfolio by setting out a shoe box, grocery bag, folder, or other holding device for collecting things at home. This is like brainstorming, only you're gathering actual samples rather than generating ideas.

Just as in brainstorming, it is important to think in the widest possible terms when creating your working portfolio. You don't want to limit yourself to school work or photos or any other single product. This exercise helps you to think broadly about what you might include as samples. It also gets you used to keeping an eye open for various kinds of samples.

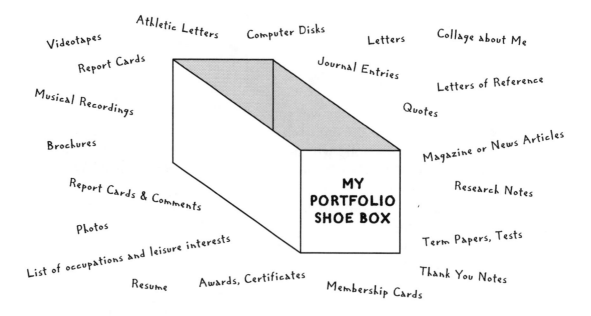

1. For each item listed below, check the box that describes your level of interest.

Album covers	☐ I collect these now	☐ I'd consider collecting these	☐ Not of interest
Artwork	☐ I collect these now	☐ I'd consider collecting these	☐ Not of interest
Athletic letters	☐ I collect these now	☐ I'd consider collecting these	☐ Not of interest
Awards or certificates	☐ I collect these now	☐ I'd consider collecting these	☐ Not of interest
Brochures	☐ I collect these now	☐ I'd consider collecting these	☐ Not of interest
Cartoons	☐ I collect these now	☐ I'd consider collecting these	☐ Not of interest

Collages or displays	☐ I collect these now	☐ I'd consider collecting these	☐ Not of interest
Compliments	☐ I collect these now	☐ I'd consider collecting these	☐ Not of interest
Computer-generated	☐ I collect these now	☐ I'd consider collecting these	☐ Not of interest
Journal or diary	☐ I collect these now	☐ I'd consider collecting these	☐ Not of interest
Letters of reference	☐ I collect these now	☐ I'd consider collecting these	☐ Not of interest
Lists	☐ I collect these now	☐ I'd consider collecting these	☐ Not of interest
Magazine articles	☐ I collect these now	☐ I'd consider collecting these	☐ Not of interest
Membership cards	☐ I collect these now	☐ I'd consider collecting these	☐ Not of interest
Multimedia projects	☐ I collect these now	☐ I'd consider collecting these	☐ Not of interest
Music	☐ I collect these now	☐ I'd consider collecting these	☐ Not of interest
Newspaper articles	☐ I collect these now	☐ I'd consider collecting these	☐ Not of interest
Notes	☐ I collect these now	☐ I'd consider collecting these	☐ Not of interest
Objects I make	☐ I collect these now	☐ I'd consider collecting these	☐ Not of interest
Photos I take	☐ I collect these now	☐ I'd consider collecting these	☐ Not of interest
Poetry	☐ I collect these now	☐ I'd consider collecting these	☐ Not of interest
Programs or fliers	☐ I collect these now	☐ I'd consider collecting these	☐ Not of interest
Puzzles	☐ I collect these now	☐ I'd consider collecting these	☐ Not of interest
Quotations	☐ I collect these now	☐ I'd consider collecting these	☐ Not of interest
Report cards	☐ I collect these now	☐ I'd consider collecting these	☐ Not of interest
Research papers	☐ I collect these now	☐ I'd consider collecting these	☐ Not of interest

Résumés	☐ I collect these now	☐ I'd consider collecting these	☐ Not of interest
Tests	☐ I collect these now	☐ I'd consider collecting these	☐ Not of interest
Thank-you notes	☐ I collect these now	☐ I'd consider collecting these	☐ Not of interest
Trading cards	☐ I collect these now	☐ I'd consider collecting these	☐ Not of interest
Videotapes	☐ I collect these now	☐ I'd consider collecting these	☐ Not of interest

2. List here three or more items you could include in your working portfolio that are not on the list.

○ _____

○ _____

○ _____

○ _____

○ _____

○ _____

A PERSONAL INVENTORY

This exercise invites you to brainstorm about who you are, what excites and motivates you, what you have to contribute, and more. As you think about yourself and your life, your mind is filled with possibilities. This mental alertness helps you to identify samples that tell your story.

Character Traits

1. List five famous people you admire. These are people you probably don't know personally but have read about or seen in magazines, on television, or in movies. Name one thing you admire about each person.

   a. Name: _____

      I admire: _____

   b. Name: _____

      I admire: _____

   c. Name: _____

      I admire: _____

   d. Name: _____

      I admire: _____

   e. Name: _____

      I admire: _____

   Look back at your list and circle one or two things you could have in common with these people.

2. List five people you admire who live in your community. These are people you know personally. They could be friends, relatives, neighbors, teachers, athletes, artists, or anyone else.

   ○ _____
   ○ _____
   ○ _____
   ○ _____
   ○ _____

a. Name one thing you admire about each person. This should be a character trait—something that makes that person special or unique.

Person   One thing I admire

✿ _____   _____

✿ _____   _____

✿ _____   _____

✿ _____   _____

✿ _____   _____

b. List two exceptional talents that one or more of these people have.

✿ _____

✿ _____

c. Describe a time when one of them took a risk for something he or she believed in.

_____

_____

_____

_____

d. Describe a time when one of them showed persistence in the face of rejection or defeat.

_____

_____

_____

_____

e. Often we admire people because they are like us, or because we have something in common with them. Look over the five names on your list of people you know personally. List two qualities you have in common with any of the people on this list.

✿ _____

✿ _____

Which of these qualities could you feature in your portfolio? How would you represent it?

_____

_____

Excellence

1. What is one thing your friends can always count on about you? Something they know you'll always do for them?

_____

Give an example to illustrate the last time you did this.

_____

_____

_____

If you were going to include this example in your portfolio, how would you do it? Could you simply describe it, write a dialogue to tell the story, use a letter or testimonial from a friend, use photos or recordings, or include a sample of your skill? Write one way you might handle this in your portfolio.

_____

_____

_____

2. Compliments make us feel good because they usually mean that someone has recognized our talents. Most of us get compliments from other people from time to time. It's important to know that compliments can take many different forms. Some examples:

- A verbal thank-you for a job well done
- A written note complimenting you on a school assignment
- A thank-you note
- A request for your help ("Could you show me how to _____?")
- Being given more responsibility on the job or in a class
- Finding out that people have been telling others about your talents ("I heard that you're good at _____. Could you do me a favor and _____?")

Listing different ways you have been complimented can help you to recognize talents you have. You may want to include samples of these talents in your portfolio. Give examples of compliments you have received in the last three months in each of the following categories.

a. Someone at school (in a classroom, in the lunchroom, on a team, or somewhere else) complimented me about:

_____

_____

b. Someone in my family or neighborhood complimented me by asking for my help in doing:

_____

_____

c. Someone I don't know very well (or a stranger) thanked me for:

_____

_____

OR asked for my help in doing:

_____

_____

Affiliations and Memberships

We all belong to groups of one kind or another. Sometimes these groups are formal—teams, clubs, associations, troops, cadres, organizations. Sometimes they are informal—just people we like to hang out with.

1. List one or more *informal* groups you belong to.

_____

_____

_____

What are these groups known for?

_____

_____

_____

What talents or interests do you need to fit into these groups?

_____

_____

_____

2. List one or more *formal* groups you belong to.

_____

_____

_____

What are these groups known for?

_____

_____

_____

What talents or interests do you use as a member of these groups?

_____

_____

_____

_____

3. List samples you could include in your portfolio to demonstrate talents you use as a member of these informal or formal groups.

   ✿   _____

   ✿   _____

   ✿   _____

   ✿   _____

Personal Challenges

Sometimes our true character comes out when we are challenged. In fact, in many cultures the rite of passage into adulthood is based on a young person facing a personal challenge.

✿ In some cultures, a young person goes out into the wilderness or jungle to survive on his or her own. By meeting this challenge, the young person knows that he or she can face anything in the future.

✿ In other cultures, young people leave home to live on their own and develop a personal vision. This may help them grasp the direction of their lives, define who they are, or come to know what they stand for.

Today, you are faced with survival in a complex world. Each challenge you meet (a tough class, a difficult relationship, a trying job search) gives you increased confidence to decide your own fate and determine the path of your own future.

1. Check any statement that describes a challenge you have faced.

   ☐ Moving to a new home and learning about a new community

   ☐ Enduring teasing or taunting by others

   ☐ Camping or living in the wilderness

   ☐ Visiting a strange new place or large city

   ☐ Changing schools and having to make new friends

   ☐ Surviving changes in your family

   ☐ Overcoming temptations to do something you know you probably shouldn't do

   ☐ Completing a tough course or assignment

   ☐ Teaching yourself to do something that others thought you never could do

2. Describe another challenge you faced and overcame.

    _____

    _____

    What talents or abilities did you use to meet the challenge?

    _____

    _____

    _____

    What sample of these talents might you include in a portfolio?

    _____

    _____

Work and Leisure

1. When was the last time you earned money, a special privilege, or a reward? This, too, is recognition of a talent you used.

    Describe what you did to earn money, a special privilege, or a reward.

    _____

    _____

    What sample of this talent might you include in a portfolio?

    _____

    _____

2. List three occupations you might like to know more about.

    ✪ _____

    ✪ _____

    ✪ _____

    What samples might you include in your portfolio related to these occupations? *Examples:* A career interest survey you completed; a copy of a job description that caught your eye.

    ✪ _____

    ✪ _____

    ✪ _____

3. The things you do in your leisure time (or would like to do) contain clues about your talents and interests. List three of your leisure interests and possible portfolio samples related to those interests. If you need help, complete the Leisure Bingo Card on page 74. It invites you to think about and list leisure activities you enjoy now or might like to explore in the future.

    a. Interest: _____

        Sample: _____

    b. Interest: _____

        Sample: _____

    c. Interest: _____

        Sample: _____

Making a Difference

What are some things you do to help others? Maybe you volunteer your time, energy, and talents to help friends, neighbors, and family members. Perhaps you get involved in community service projects. Or maybe there are volunteer activities you'd like to get involved in sometime in the future.

List three of your volunteer interests and possible portfolio samples related to each interest. If you need help, take the Volunteer Interests Inventory on pages 75–76.

    a. Interest: _____

        Sample: _____

    b. Interest: _____

        Sample: _____

    c. Interest: _____

        Sample: _____

Looking Ahead

Look ahead to the distant future, when you will be ready to retire from work. List three things you really want to do before you reach retirement age.

✪ _____

✪ _____

✪ _____

Are you working toward any of those things now? If so, consider what you might include as a sample in your portfolio.

WEEKLY PORTFOLIO LOG

WEEKLY PORTFOLIO LOG						
Sun	**Mon**	**Tue**	**Wed**	**Thur**	**Fri**	**Sat**

What's the greatest danger threatening your portfolio? Procrastination! Don't put off collecting samples until the last minute. If you take a few moments each week to think about what you want to include, then take the time to find a sample and put it in your shoe box, your portfolio will be much easier to complete.

The Portfolio Log on pages 32–34 will help to keep you on track. Set a time each week to work through it. After you have collected three or more samples, stir through your shoe box as if you were stirring through old memories. This will give you more ideas for samples you might want to include.

If your portfolio guidelines ask you to include general samples from a project, examples of personal growth, or demonstrations of general learning and expertise, use the General Samples part of the log to help you identify experiences which could be included in your portfolio. If your guidelines ask you to include specific items, use the Specific Samples part of the log to help you review the requirements. You may want to use both parts so you're sure not to forget anything.

**DO NOT GO ON TO STEP TWO
UNTIL YOU HAVE COLLECTED AND CATALOGED
AT LEAST TEN SAMPLES!**

NOTE

Every item you add to your working portfolio should be cataloged for future reference. Otherwise it's easy to forget why you put a particular item in your shoe box.

You will need to write a brief description of each item, then attach it to the item. (Try removable tape.) Each description should include the following information:

1. The name of the item (or title, or brief descriptive phrase).

2. The date it was done.

3. Some background on the item. You might include information about any of these:

   ✿ What you did or contributed

   ✿ Who you worked with

   ✿ What you had to learn or master as a skill

   ✿ Obstacles, frustrations, or challenges you faced

4. A reason why you are including it as a sample. Answer any of these questions:

   ✿ What did you learn about yourself as a result of the experience related to the sample?

   ✿ What abilities or interests does this sample reveal about you?

   ✿ What does this sample tell about you?

5. Any other important dates or other information related to the item.

PORTFOLIO LOG

Week of_____

General Samples

Experiences that demonstrate your expertise, personal growth, and accomplishments

1. What have you done in the past or recently that makes you proud? What have you enjoyed? Check any statement that is true for you:

    ☐ I received a compliment, was asked to help someone, or got a nice note (or grade) on an assignment

    ☐ I did something useful in a group I belong to

    ☐ I was able to meet a personal challenge or took the first step to meeting that challenge

    ☐ I earned some money, a privilege, or a reward

    ☐ I've thought about a possible occupation

    ☐ I really enjoyed my leisure time

    ☐ I helped out or volunteered

    ☐ I learned something about myself

    ☐ An unusual thing happened

    ☐ I improved in a skill (in class, at home, on a team, etc.) or learned a new skill

    ☐ Other: _____

2. Describe in detail anything you checked. Add more pages for writing if you need them.

    _____
    _____
    _____
    _____
    _____
    _____
    _____
    _____
    _____
    _____
    _____
    _____
    _____
    _____

Specific Samples

Required items for your portfolio

Review Exercise 2: Brainstorming about Student Portfolios—Specific List on pages 15–17.

1. Describe one required item and a sample you might use to meet the requirement.

   Required item: _____

   Sample: _____

2. Describe something you are working on now (or will complete in the near future) that you might use to meet a requirement.

   Required item: _____

   Sample: _____

Preparing Your Samples

Check and complete anything you need to do to prepare each sample you are adding to your working portfolio.

☐ If you can't put the actual sample in your working portfolio:

   Make a copy of the original

   Take a picture of the sample

   Scan a photograph

   Other: _____

Notes about specific samples: _____

_____

_____

_____

☐ Collect: _____

☐ Make or display something to represent the sample. *Examples:* make a collage, complete a display, assemble equipment, etc. Describe what you need to do. _____

_____

_____

☐ Ask for permission to: _____

_____

_____

☐ Go and get: _____

_____

_____

☐ Something else you need to do: _____

_____

_____

NOTES: _____

_____

_____

_____

_____

_____

_____

_____

_____

_____

_____

_____

_____

_____

_____

_____

_____

_____

_____

_____

_____

_____

Selecting and Organizing Your Samples

A fter your working portfolio is full of possible samples, it's time to select the best ones to include in your final portfolio. You'll start by considering your audience. Who will be viewing your portfolio? Teachers, parents, employers, college admissions personnel, committees, community representatives, peers, or...? What will your audience be looking for? Have you been given a list of specific items to include—items your audience expects or needs to see?

Next, you'll group your samples and put them in order. You'll give each item a title, description or caption, and page number (if you choose). Finally, you'll add the front matter, typically a title page, table of contents, and introduction. You may want to provide a Highlights Summary, described on pages 64–65. At the end of your portfolio, you may want to include a summary statement analyzing and evaluating your portfolio and the experience of creating a portfolio.

BRAINSTORMING ABOUT YOUR AUDIENCE

Before you can create your final portfolio, you must answer three important questions:

- ☼ "Who is going to see my portfolio?"
- ☼ "What will they look for?"
- ☼ "How will they evaluate my portfolio?"

You might know the answers in advance, or you might have to guess the answers. Either way, this exercise will help you to decide what your portfolio should include. You should try to describe *at least three* potential types of audience members. Make at least three copies of the Audience Worksheet on page 37. Then do the evaluation activity on page 38.

NOTE

If you are creating a personal portfolio, you can skip this exercise because you are the audience.

Audience Worksheet

1. Assume that you are required to show your portfolio to certain types of people. *Examples:* teachers, counselors, other students, community representatives, college admissions officers, bank loan officers, contest judges. Name one type here.

   _____

   a. Describe an important quality or skill that type of person might look for in your portfolio. *Examples:* responsibility, knowledge, motivation, growth, attitude, a specific skill.

   _____

   b. Write a question they might ask you.

   _____

   c. Describe a sample they might look for.

   _____

   d. Describe something else they might expect to see.

   _____

2. Assume that you can invite anyone you choose to see your portfolio. *Examples:* a favorite coach, teacher, minister, supervisor, friend, uncle, grandmother, neighbor, counselor. Name one person here.

   _____

   a. Describe an important quality or skill that person might look for in your portfolio. *Examples:* responsibility, knowledge, motivation, growth, attitude, a specific skill.

   _____

   b. Write a question that person might ask you.

   _____

   c. Describe a sample he or she might look for.

   _____

   d. Describe something else he or she might expect to see.

   _____

Evaluation

Some portfolios are judged and compared with other portfolios. You might know in advance exactly how your portfolio will be evaluated, or you might have to work only with general guidelines.

1. Imagine that you're in charge of designing a form for evaluating portfolios. You have identified and described two qualities you would look for—completeness and neatness. What other qualities would you want to see? How would you define them? Finish the form.

PORTFOLIO EVALUATION FORM

Demonstrates the following qualities	Experienced 1	Skilled 2	Entry Level 3
Completeness	10 or more samples	5–9 samples	1–4 samples
Neatness	Clean, easy to view	Somewhere in between	Messy or sloppy

2. If you have been given a list of criteria, write them here.

a. _____

b. _____

c. _____

d. _____

e. _____

f. _____

SELECTING YOUR SAMPLES

Based on what you learned from Exercise 6, list the samples you plan to include in your final portfolio. You don't have to list them in any particular order at this time.

_____

_____

_____

_____

_____

_____

_____

_____

_____

_____

_____

_____

_____

_____

_____

_____

_____

_____

_____

_____

_____

_____

_____

_____

_____

_____

_____

_____

_____

ANALYZING YOUR SAMPLES

What important qualities and skills do your samples represent? What do they communicate about your talents and abilities? You can find out by analyzing your samples with a coding system known as DPT.

The United States Department of Labor has determined that all of the jobs in the U.S. can be put into one large *Dictionary of Occupational Titles* (DOT). Each job is described and classified in terms of three types of skills: Data, People, and Things (DPT). Each type of skill is broken down into several specific skills that are ranked from highest to lowest, as shown on the following chart. Then each job is rated or coded with a number from each skill area.

DPT SKILLS
From highest to lowest

Data (Information)	People	Things
0 Synthesizing	0 Mentoring	0 Setting up equipment
1 Coordinating	1 Negotiating	1 Precision working
2 Analyzing	2 Instructing	2 Operating/ controlling
3 Compiling	3 Supervising	3 Driving/operating
4 Computing	4 Diverting	4 Manipulating
5 Copying	5 Persuading	5 Tending to equipment/things
6 Comparing	6 Speaking/Signaling	6 Feeding/operating
	7 Serving	7 Handling things
	8 Taking Instructions/Helping	

Study the following chart and see if you can tell why each job is rated as shown.

DPT SCORES

Job	Data	People	Things
Psychologist	1	0	7
Nurse (LPN)	3	7	4
Carpenter	3	8	4
Chemist	2	6	1
Arc Welder	6	1	0
Logger	6	8	4

Most jobs have one or two skills that stand out or rank highest. These are the *lowest* numbers. For instance, a psychologist must coordinate data in reports (1) and have excellent people skills (0). A carpenter must be able to interpret blueprints and measure accurately (3) and manipulate tools and materials (4). The logger must be able to use tools out in the woods (4) but doesn't require high level people skills (8).

You may not agree with each DPT score because your work experience or knowledge of a particular job might be different. Still, DPT scores are useful because they show what kinds of skills are *generally* needed on the job. Most jobs typically require all three types of skills, with one or two emphasized more than the other(s).

1. Look at the list of jobs on the following chart. Which *two* types of skills do you think are most important for each one? Indicate your choices with X's in the appropriate columns. The first job, "Tailor," has been done for you as an example. If you need help with the others, ask yourself:

    ✿ "What would this person's job duties be most often?"

    ✿ "If I were hiring someone to do this job, which two types of skills would be most important?"

WHAT'S THE SCORE?

Job	Data	People	Things
Tailor		X	X
Flower arranger			
Miner			
Ice cream truck driver			
Teacher			
Biologist			
Animal trainer			
Farmer			
Counselor			
Secretary			
Cashier			
Lifeguard			

2. What do *you* prefer most, working with Data, People, or Things? What do your portfolio samples tell you? List your samples on the following chart. Which *two* types of skills do you think are most important for each one? Indicate your choices with X's in the appropriate columns. Then add up the number of X's in each column.

ANALYZE YOUR SAMPLES WITH DPT

Samples	Data	People	Things
1			
2			
3			
4			
5			
6			
7			
8			
9			
10			
11			
12			
13			
14			
15			
TOTALS			

Were you surprised by the totals? Why or why not?

_____

_____

Based on your analysis, would you like to make any changes to the list of samples you selected for your portfolio? Go back to Exercise 7 on page 39 and review your list. Add, subtract, or substitute samples to make your portfolio accurately represent who you really are and what you want to become.

Organizing Your Samples

There are six basic ways to organize your samples. Read the following descriptions, then choose the one that seems to fit your needs. Discuss your choice with someone else to get feedback.

1. According to Instructions

You may not have a choice. If you were given a list of items to include and instructions on how to organize them, then follow the instructions exactly.

2. In Chronological Order

Very straightforward. Make sure all of your samples are dated, then organize them from earliest to most recent.

3. By Level of Complexity

Start with simple samples and progress to more complex ones. For instance, you may want to show how you have grown in a skill or ability. You'll begin with samples of your first attempts. (*Examples:* Records of early timings in track events, first essays in an English class, early math assignments, recordings of your first performances on a musical instrument.) Later in your portfolio, you'll include samples showing how you have improved. Typically, this method is chronological.

4. By Talents, Skills, or Areas of Knowledge

If your portfolio shows a variety of talents, skills, and knowledge areas, you might want to organize it with DPT. Label three folders "Data," "People," and "Things." Then put each of your samples in the folder that best represents the type of skill used to create it. If a sample is too big to put in a folder, write its name on a 3x5 card and put the card in the folder.

If your portfolio emphasizes a particular set of talents, you probably should try a different approach.

- To demonstrate your leadership or managerial skills, you might organize your samples under "Managing People," "Data," "Projects," and "Finances."

- If you are interested in a theatrical career, you might organize your samples under "Acting," "Directing," "Stage Crafts," "Publicity," and/or "Writing."

- If your portfolio is about a hobby, think about what goes into it. For instance, model railroading involves design, artistic talents, electrical skills, and construction.

Organizing your portfolio by talents may prove very helpful when you need to write a résumé or complete a college application.

5. By Theme

Perhaps you are taking a class or series of classes that have a theme. *Examples:* "Becoming a Technologically Literate Citizen," "People Interacting with the Environment." You might choose a theme for your portfolio and create categories within that theme.

⚙ For a portfolio on "People Interacting with the Environment," you might group samples by the following three categories: "Research into Environmental Issues," "Community Projects to Improve the Environment," and "Technologies and Materials Used to Conserve and Improve the Environment."

You may want to develop your own themes or thematic groupings. Look over your samples and group the ones that seem to have something in common.

⚙ Which samples show how you have grown as a person? You might group them together under "Personal Growth."

⚙ Which samples show a challenge you have met? You might name this group "Personal Challenges" or "Risk Taking."

⚙ Which ones show membership in different groups? You might organize these as "Memberships," "Affiliations," and "Contributions."

6. Combination Options

What if you combine Themes with Talents? You might start by organizing your samples by three themes: "Community Service," "Preparing for Work," and "Leisure." Then, within each group, you could organize your samples further by talents. By combining two or more different ways to organize your samples, you can come up with something truly original.

OUTLINING YOUR PORTFOLIO

EXERCISE 9

1. Consider the different ways of organizing your samples, then check the method or methods you plan to use.

    ☐   According to instructions

    ☐   In chronological order

    ☐   By level of complexity

    ☐   By talents, skills, or areas of knowledge

    ☐   By theme

    ☐   Combination options _____ and _____

2. Study the outlines shown below and on pages 46–48. Circle the letter of the outline that gives you the best ideas for organizing your samples.

A. Chronological Outline
Accomplishments for My School Career

I. The Beginning Year 1997-1998
    A. Early average to poor attendance
    B. Early transcripts
    C. List of a club and a sport I was involved with

II. The Growing Years 1998-2001
    A. Recent good attendance record
    B. Recent transcripts
    C. List of clubs attended and athletic awards won
    D. Article about my club's food shelter project
    E. Letters of reference

III. Goals for the Future Beyond 2001
    A. Career goals
    B. Career report about duties, qualifications, schools
    C. College goals
    D. College brochures
    E. Personal goals

IV. Self-Evaluation

    A. Journal: "Who Am I? Where Am I Going?"

B. Talents Outline
Work and Leisure Talents Portfolio

I. Career Talents
    A. Vocational classes
    B. Marketing class project

II. Leadership Roles
    A. Vocational Industrial Clubs of America (VICA) accomplishment
    B. Samples from my VICA treasurer's reports
    C. Photos showing my participation in the three-day conference, "Business Week"

III. Arts & Music Contributions
    A. Models of a set designed for a school play
    B. Woodworking awards from local club
    C. Photo of display at all-city crafts show
    D. Membership card from Junior Symphony

IV. Journal Evaluation
    A. What I learned from making a portfolio
    D. What I hope to be doing in 5 years

C. Thematic Outline
Life & Learning Path

I. Learning about Myself
    A. Journal entries
    B. First term paper I earned an "A" on
    C. Description of personal challenge in my family (Dad's unemployment)

II. Learning about My Community and My Values
    A. Work experiences (beginning wage, ending wage, letter of reference)
    B. My church (sheet music from choir, picture of us singing in nursing home)
    C. Friendships (information about the exchange student program)

III. Expressing Myself
    A. Poetry reprinted from school publication
    B. Letter to the editor
    C. Video still printed from a videotape
    D. Poster done for fundraiser (photo)

IV. Special Moments
    A. Debate club in French class
    B. Directing the Talent Show
    C. At my favorite get-away place (poem and photo)

V. Closing Thoughts
    A. Enduring themes in my life

D. Combination Outline:
Chronological and Thematic
Life & Learning Path

I. Early Explorations of Myself and My Community
    A. Freshman year transcript and summary of my most important class
    B. Volunteer work (science class stream cleanup)
    C. First exposure to drama (stage hand in school play)

II. My Sense of Self (Latest Accomplishments)
    A. List of various clubs and offices I hold
    B. Articles about teams I play on in the community (soccer, track)
    C. Science fair award and subsequent scholarship

III. My Dilemma for the Future
    A. Letter inviting me to join Washington's Volunteer Service Corps
    B. Letter of acceptance to college
    C. Invitation to winter internship in state government
    D. A picture I'll draw showing the three choices and my confusion about which offer to take

3. Create an outline for your portfolio. Start with a rough draft, then revise it until you have a final outline that works for you. Write your final outline on page 50.

Rough Draft Outline

Type of outline: _____

Title:_____

I. _____

   A. _____

   B. _____

   C. _____

   D. _____

II. _____

   A. _____

   B. _____

   C. _____

   D. _____

III. _____

   A. _____

   B. _____

   C. _____

   D. _____

IV. _____

   A. _____

   B. _____

   C. _____

   D. _____

Final Outline

Type of outline: _____

Title:_____

I.   _____
  A.   _____
  B.   _____
  C.   _____
  D.   _____

II.   _____
  A.   _____
  B.   _____
  C.   _____
  D.   _____

III. _____
  A.   _____
  B.   _____
  C.   _____
  D.   _____

IV.   _____
  A.   _____
  B.   _____
  C.   _____
  D.   _____

Adding Titles and Descriptions

Once you've selected and organized your samples, it's time to give each one a title and description. Without this important information, your audience might not understand why you included a particular sample.

For instance, a letter of reference or award certificate might explain itself. But what about a union card, a student I.D. card, or a copy of your driver's license? Perhaps the union card shows your ability to assume an adult role in the work world, where you earned union membership by working in a factory or hospital. A student I.D. card might be used to tell the story of your participation in fundraising, student committees, or outstanding attendance. Maybe you've given up driving a car and now ride a bike to help reduce pollution, and that's why you put a copy of your driver's license in your portfolio. In other words, you have excellent reasons for selecting these samples, but your audience won't know your reasons unless you include them in your descriptions.

What about an athletic letter, followed by a report card, followed by a student I.D. card? What does it all mean? What about a science quiz with a C-minus grade? Will your audience know that you included the C-minus paper to illustrate your growth into a B-plus student? Not unless you tell them.

○ Titles should be short and simple.

○ Descriptions (also called captions) should be detailed, powerful, and convincing.

Below are two sample portfolio pages about the same experience. Which one would you include in your portfolio?

MY 100-MILE BIKE TRIP

I rode from Redwood City to Big Sur in one day with 4 other people. It was a grueling challenge, and one I would like to do again. We are planning more trips for next summer.

MY 100-MILE BIKE TRIP

A 4-person team of students planned a 100-mile bike ride from Redwood City to Big Sur campgrounds. I was responsible for coordinating the meals and planning the route. I consulted with everyone before coming up with a plan. The entire planning took 4 months and we have been asked to present our experience to other bike teams. I learned a lot about leadership and persistence.

The more details you include, the better your audience will understand the importance of your sample and why you chose to include it. A convincing description can get results—a good grade, offers of advice or help, letters of reference, recommendations to prospective employers or college admissions deans.

○ The students who created the bike riding portfolio (and included the more detailed sample page) took their portfolio to a banker when they wanted a loan to set up a bike repair and tour guide business. They got their loan.

WRITING BASIC DESCRIPTIONS

1. Choose five samples that are most important to you. These are the samples for which you will write descriptions. List them here. (You may be instructed to choose specific samples, and to choose more than five. This exercise will get you started.)

○ _____

○ _____

○ _____

○ _____

○ _____

A basic description includes five elements.

a. A title.

Example: "Contributing to the Outdoors: Preparing for a Career in Landscaping"

b. Information about the sample.

Answer questions like these: Who did you work with? What tools or materials did you use? How long did it take? What research or independent study did you accomplish? Who helped you? What challenges, frustrations, or problems did you face?

Example: "I worked on an outdoor crew cleaning streams and clearing trails. We worked in crews of 5 people and began work when the sun first came up. Oftentimes it was cold. We had to haul tools and gravel to make the bridge and handicapped accessible path. The 2-mile trail took 400 hours of work to complete."

c. An explanation of why this sample is important to you.

Why did you include it in your portfolio?

Example: "This was important to me because it was my first paid job. Also, I found out that I like to work outdoors. It gave me a great sense of satisfaction. I often go back to the trail and just stare at my handiwork. I know that no matter what else I might do in my life, the trail will always be there. I chose to include this as a sample of my work habits."

d. An explanation of something you might do differently if you could repeat the experience.

Is there anything you would improve?

Example: "There is nothing I would improve. However, if I ever did something like this again, I would take pictures for a scrapbook."

e.   A reason why this sample might be important to your audience.

What impression will they form about you, based on this sample? TIP: Show your sample to someone you like and trust. Share your title, information, and why the sample is important to you. Ask the person, "What does this sample tell you about my attitudes, abilities, interests, and character? What kind of impression does it give you about me?"

Example: "I think my audience will look at my sample and see that I am mature and hard-working. They will be impressed that I took the time to make a contribution."

2.   Make five copies of the Sample Description Worksheet on page 55, then create basic descriptions for the five samples you chose. Get feedback when you're done. If you're creating your portfolio for school, show your descriptions to the teacher. If you're creating your portfolio for other reasons, show your descriptions to someone who knows you well or who might be interested in seeing your final portfolio. Use the feedback to improve your descriptions.

Sample Description Worksheet

a. Title: _____

b. Information: _____

_____

_____

_____

_____

_____

_____

_____

c. Why important to me: _____

_____

_____

_____

_____

d. What I might do differently/improve: _____

_____

_____

_____

_____

_____

e. Why important to my audience: _____

_____

_____

_____

_____

_____

ENRICHING YOUR DESCRIPTIONS

Sometimes it's hard to find just the right words to make your descriptions powerful and impressive. On pages 77–79 you'll find four word lists that can help you to enrich your descriptions. The first three include words specific to Data, People, and Things (see pages 40–42). The fourth includes words describing character traits, temperaments, work habits, and self-management skills.

You'll need five copies of the Enriching Your Descriptions Worksheet on page 58, one for each sample you described in Exercise 10.

1. For each sample you described in Exercise 10, list four skills you used to create it or complete it. Use words from lists 1–3 on pages 77–78. Use the categories (Data, People, Things) as guidelines, but don't let them limit you. For instance, there may be a word on the Data list that describes a skill you used with People or Things.

    Example: "This sample is mostly about working with *things* and *people.* I believe that it demonstrates the following skills:

    Designed solutions for trail and bridge work.

    Minimized risks by working safely, especially with power equipment.

    Operated power blowers, chain saws, and pneumatic hammers safely.

    Negotiated with others—secured permission from a nearby farmer to build a bridge in the park."

2. For each sample you described in Exercise 10, list four character traits, temperaments, work habits, and/or self-management skills you used to create it or complete it. Use words from list 4 on pages 78–79.

    Example: "This sample demonstrates that I'm a *team player, mature, diplomatic, inventive,* and *energetic.*"

3. Can you add words that quantify your results or efforts? Audiences like numbers. When you say, "I recruited 50 new players," "I increased customer satisfaction 20 percent," "I spent 25 hours in community service," or "I helped to reduce errors from 15 a day to 4 a day," people know exactly what you mean.

    For each sample you described in Exercise 10, try to add words or numbers that show a quantity or a degree of change. Ask yourself questions like:

    ✿ How long did it take? How many hours, days, months?

    ✿ Did I increase something positive? (Number of customers, compliments, requests, contacts, etc.?) Did I decrease something negative? (Number of complaints, rejections, returns, discards, disagreements, requests for help, etc.?)

    ✿ How often was something done? Every day, week, month? How many times a day, week, month?

- How efficiently did you work?
- How many people, things, or groups were involved?
- How much data did you use? What kinds? From how many sources?
- Can you describe anything in terms of percentages, probabilities, report results, or survey results?

Example: "Since we improved the trail, the number of visitors to the park has gone from 200 a week to 400 a week."

Enriching Your Descriptions Worksheet

Sample: _____

DPT Skills

⚙ _____

⚙ _____

⚙ _____

⚙ _____

Character Traits

⚙ _____

⚙ _____

⚙ _____

⚙ _____

Numbers

⚙ _____

⚙ _____

⚙ _____

⚙ _____

FINALIZING YOUR DESCRIPTIONS

For this exercise, you'll need:

- ✿ writing paper
- ✿ whatever you will be using for your final portfolio "pages." See Choosing a Format on page 61.

To create your final descriptions, look back at the work you did in exercises 10 and 11. Take your best words, sentences, and phrases. Write, then revise and write again until your descriptions are the best they can be. If possible, get feedback from others.

Place your titles and descriptions consistently throughout your portfolio. You might create them on a computer or use rub-off letters for a professional appearance. The examples below show one way you might choose to arrange your sample pages: title at the top, sample in the middle, description at the bottom.

GETTING AROUND

I used to drive to school and everywhere else I went. As a result of my environmental studies, I've given up driving because it causes pollution. I now ride a bike to school and most other places I go. When I need to travel farther than I can ride my bike, I take the bus or ride share.

MEETING THE SCIENCE CHALLENGE

Science has always been a difficult subject for me. Here you see my first test, a C-. By putting in 5 hours a week in the after-school study hall, I was able to earn an A on the semester test, included on the next page of my portfolio. My final grade for the semester was a B+.

NOTE

You have three options when it comes to finalizing your descriptions.

1. Create a title and description for each sample, then put them on the page with the sample, as shown in the examples above.

2. Organize your samples into groups, then create a title and description for each group. Your description should explain why you grouped the samples. You probably will want to put your title and description on a separate page preceding your group of samples.

3. Create a title and description for each sample, then put them on a separate page. The sample will follow on its own page. This works best for portfolios containing ten or fewer samples.

Choosing a Format

How do you want your final portfolio to look? You have several choices, depending on the samples your portfolio contains and the resources available to you.

○ The simplest, most popular (and traditional) format is a binder or scrapbook. You organize your samples and descriptions within the binder or scrapbook, like a book with pages.

○ If you use computers to scan materials (illustrations, photographs, artwork) and a video camera to record specific events, you may want to put your entire portfolio on a computer disk. Your portfolio then becomes a multimedia presentation.

○ If your portfolio includes three-dimensional objects, you may want to keep them in a box. Put your descriptions in order in a binder or scrapbook. Give your samples and descriptions the same numbers for easy reference.

High-tech, low-tech, or no-tech...it really doesn't matter. What matters most is that your samples are well-chosen, well-organized, and well-described in a way that tells your story.

Should You Add Page Numbers?

Some people do, and some people don't. You may be required to add page numbers, or you may have a choice. If you have a choice, keep this in mind: Some people keep their portfolios for a long time—years, even decades. They continue to add new samples as they grow and develop new interests. Eventually they take out some samples and place them in a long-term storage box for safekeeping.

It's easier to add and remove samples if pages are *not* numbered. It's also easier to move pages around to meet the needs of different audiences.

If you want your portfolio to change as you change, keep it flexible. Don't add page numbers unless you must. If you must add page numbers, you may want to make them removable.

Adding Front Matter

Cover or Title Page

Your title might be a descriptive phrase or thematic statement that describes what your portfolio tells about you. Or it can be as simple as "(Your Name's) Portfolio." Even if you use your name in the title, you still need to list yourself as the author.

Your title page might also include the date your portfolio was completed; the class, school, or group you submitted it to; and a statement thanking the people who helped you with your portfolio project. This statement is called the "Acknowledgments."

Example:

"I wish to acknowledge the following people and organizations:

- ⚙ Mrs. Krantzmeyer, for her assistance in editing my work

- ⚙ Mr. Ovaldorf, who helped me to digitize or computer scan several of my samples

- ⚙ My parents, for all the summer classes they took me to which helped me discover who I am

- ⚙ My football team, which taught me a valuable lesson about life, as shown in this portfolio."

Table of Contents

Try to keep this to one page. You may be able to list every sample, or you may only have room to list general areas covered in your portfolio. You must create a table of contents even if your portfolio pages are not numbered. Be sure to list your Introduction or Highlights Summary (described on pages 64–65) and any important back matter (see pages 66–68).

Introduction

Your portfolio deserves an introduction. An introduction is like a letter to your audience, telling them what they are about to see and why. Some people begin their introduction with the words "Dear Reader."

You'll want to be sure to write your introduction *after* you have finalized your portfolio. It's important to stand back and look at your entire portfolio before trying to describe it to your audience. If you need help writing your introduction, follow the outline. (As an alternative to a formal introduction, you may want to create a Portfolio Highlights Summary, described on pages 64–65.)

I. **Tell about yourself.**

A. Where you are from; your age; words that describe you (see vocabulary list 4 on pages 78–79 for ideas).

Example: "I grew up in the Pacific Northwest. I am completing this portfolio in my senior year at Timberland High School. I could be described as a person who is casual, sincere, and self-reliant."

B. A highlight or important quality in your life; things or experiences that define and shape your life; something that makes you *you.*

Example: "Being a 'military brat' probably shaped my life in many ways. We were always moving, and as a result I had to learn how to fit in and rely on myself."

C. What's important to you: your values, work habits, time, health, accomplishments, contributions, interests, safety, etc.

Example: "Stability and family are important to me. I value having reliable friends and being seen as a dependable person. My strongest work habit could be described as follow-through, whether at home or school or on a team. I love sports and music. I find great satisfaction in having earned a varsity soccer letter. I also enjoy working with others on important projects."

D. Where you are going next in life; your goals.

   Example: "My next goal in life is to determine how I can best support myself. At the moment, I am considering going to work right after I graduate from high school and taking a few courses at the community college to see what I am interested in."

II. Describe some of the highlights of your portfolio.

A. Identify some of the most important samples in your portfolio. List two or three that mean the most to you.

B. Tell why these samples are important to you. What about them matters? Tell why you are proud of these achievements. What extra effort did you make? What did you learn about yourself and your world?

C. In a few sentences, describe what your portfolio demonstrates about you. (You may already have done this in A and B.)

Example: "The fire starter kit I used once while lost in the forest is perhaps the most important sample in my entire portfolio. It shows that I can survive by my wits. These were skills I learned on my own, and they give me a real sense of confidence and security."

III. Tell what you have learned about yourself as a result of creating your portfolio.

TIP: For additional ideas and suggestions, see pages 66–68. You can use these questions for back matter *and* front matter, or for front matter instead of back matter.

A. How would you summarize the experience? What has it meant to you?

B. Did you notice some new connections in your life? Relationships between events and things that weren't obvious before?

C. Do you see a link between your past and future experiences?

D. Have you developed any new outlooks about school, work, people, success, or any other topic touched on in your portfolio?

Example: "At first my portfolio was just a collection of different things I enjoyed. But as I put my samples in order, I began to realize that I am a person who is most at home when I am around others or when others are relying on me.... As the pages fell into sequence, I saw how my early classes challenged me to work hard just to get passing grades. I now see that the excellence I achieved on the soccer field and the skills I learned in my more difficult classes resulted from the same thing: dedication. I am confident that I can profit from college, once I discover what it is I want to dedicate my life to."

Portfolio Highlights Summary

A Highlights Summary is similar to a résumé. You choose the samples that mean the most to you personally, then list and describe them, as shown in the example on page 65.

○ List highlights in the left-hand column. Keep your descriptions short. Use bold type for emphasis.

○ Describe highlights in the right-hand column. Begin each description with the skill or talent you used or demonstrated. Underline the skill or talent for emphasis. Add a few details. Include dates and locations if relevant.

○ Your summary should fit on one side of a single page.

Your completed exercises 10 and 11 contain many of the words and ideas you'll need to create your Highlights Summary.

Portfolio Highlights Summary

Samples Included	*Talents Demonstrated*
Future Farmers of America (FFA) Award	<u>Leadership skills</u> and a strong interest in farming and taking care of the land resulted in this award, given at the 1995 State Conference in Spokane, Washington.
Report Cards	<u>Academic skills.</u> Honors student with a 3.8 GPA.
Cassette Tape	<u>Musical abilities</u> are demonstrated in an original song written for a fundraising drive and awareness campaign. Fall 1997.
Term Paper	<u>Critical thinking and research skills</u> went into this report about local watershed problems. The report helped us develop a stream clean-up project as part of the Future Farmers of America. Spring 1998.
Science Log	<u>Scientific investigation methods</u> were mastered in this organic chemistry class.
Community Service Brochure	<u>Learning about the community</u> was involved in creating this listing of emergency services for kids, operated by kids. The brochure was later used in a local crisis center. Winter 1996.
Collage	<u>Self-knowledge</u> was the basis of creating this collage in my Home and Family Life course on personal development. It depicts my personal values and cultural heritage.
Poem in Spanish	<u>Pride in my cultural roots</u> is demonstrated in this poem about my family. 1997.
Peer Tutoring Certificate	<u>Listening and counseling abilities</u> were demonstrated in this program. 1996.

Adding Back Matter

Any experience is more meaningful if you reflect on it afterward. Spend some time thinking about your portfolio experience. What has it taught you about yourself, your learning, your talents? How has it benefited you? If you did it again in the future, what might you do differently?

Look over the following questions to find ideas or topics you may want to cover in your concluding statement. Your statement should fit on one side of a single page.

NOTE

A concluding self-evaluation statement only belongs in a student or school portfolio. Do not include this statement if you plan to present your portfolio to an employer, funding agency, or customer. However, you can still write a statement for your personal use and benefit.

1. Analyzing Your Content

a. Why did you select certain samples?

b. How did you get started on your portfolio? Did anyone help you to create your portfolio? Who?

c. Which samples are your best or favorite pieces? Tell why they are effective or important.

d. Which samples did you learn the most from? Tell why.

e. Describe a particular sample in detail, telling:

   ○ what you liked most about the experience represented by the sample

   ○ where you got information and advice

   ○ what frustrated you most about the experience

   ○ what you would do differently next time

f. As you look back at your portfolio, are you surprised at what you included?

g. What is something you seem to be consistently good at, as demonstrated in your portfolio?

h. What talents do your samples demonstrate?

i. Which samples in your portfolio match your career interests? Explain the connection in detail.

2. Analyzing Your Learning

a. How do some of your samples demonstrate your use of previous learning?

b. What should an evaluator look for when grading this portfolio?

c. What types of learning do you seem to like best?

d. What is one area of learning that still makes you nervous or challenges you?

e. Choose the most important sample in your portfolio. Tell what you learned from this experience.

f. Do you prefer to learn in classes or on your own?

g. What is something you'd really like to learn about next?

h. Do you think you have you become too specialized in a given area? What do you need to do to broaden your outlook?

i. What areas do you want to continue learning about on your own? How will you go about doing that?

3. Analyzing Yourself

a. How does your portfolio demonstrate that you are willing to take risks?

b. Ten years from now, what would you like to be able to put in a portfolio? Which samples in your current portfolio represent things you think you'll still be interested in and/or good at in the future?

c. What are you most proud of in your life today?

d. What goals have you reached, as demonstrated by your portfolio?

e. What is the biggest challenge or change you have had to face in order to improve or become more successful?

f. If you were asked to summarize the person described by your portfolio, what word, phrase, or quotation would you use? What theme or value describes your life up to this point in time?

g. Assume that you keep adding to your portfolio. What do you hope it might contain five years from now?

h. Create a cover for next year's portfolio. What art work will you include and why?

i. What symbol and quotation or slogan would you put on your portfolio cover to tell the reader about the person inside?

4. Analyzing the Portfolio Experience

a. How difficult would you say it is to make a portfolio? Would you be willing to do it again?

b. How might you change the way in which you go about making your next portfolio?

c. What grade would you give yourself on this portfolio? Justify the grade.

d. Does your portfolio really tell the whole story about you? Why or why not?

e. Is it difficult to judge your own work? Why or why not?

f. What did you learn about others as you completed this project?

Presenting Your Portfolio

t some point, you may be asked to present your portfolio to a teacher, another student, or a review board.

○ You can use material developed earlier for your outline (see Exercise 9, pages 45–50) or your Portfolio Highlights Summary (see pages 64–65) to guide your presentation.

○ Be sure to think about your audience and their interests. Then tailor your presentation to them. To review the process of analyzing your audience, look back at the Audience Worksheets you completed for Exercise 6 (see page 37). You may find it helpful to complete another Audience Worksheet now that you know who your audience will be.

○ Typically, you will want to show your best samples and comment on why they are important. You can tell your audience what talents these samples represent and what you learned from them. For ideas, look over any material you may want to include in your back matter (see pages 66–68).

○ Don't be afraid to add flash and flair to your presentation. You don't have to be a musician to include background music. You might show slides, bring in objects to be held and passed around, show graphics on an overhead projector, or hand out a business card.

Coping with the Fear of Public Speaking

Will you be nervous about presenting your portfolio? Yes. Everyone is! In fact, when people in the United States were asked to list their worst fears, public speaking was in the Top Ten—along with fear of heights, death, loneliness, insects, and mad dogs.

What's your *worst* fear about presenting your portfolio to an audience? Stop and think about it.

What's the *best* way to handle your fear? By rehearsing what you are going to say. This gives you the confidence to begin. Then, once you start speaking, you'll find that your worst fear never materializes.

Here's a list of tips you may want to try. Check any you think might help you to feel prepared and confident about giving your presentation.

GETTING READY...

☐ Rehearse. Practice. Know your material well. This shouldn't be too hard to do. After all, your portfolio is *your* story. If possible, rehearse your presentation with a friend, teacher, or family member.

☐ Imagine the questions you will hear and the compliments you might receive. Rehearse your responses in your mind.

☐ Dress up for the occasion. You'll feel more confident and professional.

☐ Prepare an outline to bring to your presentation.

RIGHT BEFORE YOU BEGIN...

☐ Take some deep breaths.

☐ Give yourself permission to be afraid, take risks...and not to worry about being perfect.

DURING YOUR PRESENTATION...

☐ Use the names of the people in your audience, if you know them.

☐ Make eye contact with your audience.

☐ Follow your outline.

☐ Be yourself. If you are a casual person, act casual. If you are a precise, more formal person, then act that way. Don't try to mimic other speakers. Your audience is there to see *you*.

Preparing for Questions

In most cases, the people in your audience are not there to grade you. They are there to listen, learn, and perhaps ask questions.

For instance, they might be impressed with your use of computers, the way you worked cooperatively on a team, the amount of time you volunteered for a service project, how you solved problems at school, your artistic samples, or your sports experiences. They might ask questions like, "How did you come up with the design for your poster?" "What kind of computer program did you use?" "Where did you get your idea for solving the problem?" "How long did it take to earn your letter in track?" They are requesting more details because they are interested in what you are saying.

Don't be afraid to ask your listeners some questions of your own. *Examples:* "Do you feel that my portfolio gives you a good picture of my efforts?" "Do you have any questions about the samples I've shown?" "Do you have any advice related to some of the conclusions or thoughts I've shared with you today?" "Have any of you ever made a portfolio? If so, what did you use it for?"

At the end of your presentation, the people in your audience might make comments acknowledging your efforts. One person might lean forward, smile, and say, "I notice in this project that you display exceptional persistence. I have found this important in my work when I get involved with community agencies. I also recognize that you must have strong feelings about helping others. Is this true?" Another might ask, "Will you try this again?" Still another might inquire, "Has your portfolio given you any ideas for future careers or volunteer work?"

When it's all over, you'll look back at your presentation and think, "That wasn't so bad." You might even think, "That was fun!"

Resources

Leisure Bingo Card

Here are 15 different categories of leisure activities, with examples. Your card is filled when each square contains at least three more ideas. Add things you enjoy now or might like to explore in the future.

ACTIVE GAMES Darts, croquet, video games _____ _____ _____ _____	ANIMALS AND PLANTS Gardening, animal care _____ _____ _____ _____	SPIRITUAL, CULTURAL Religion, metaphysics _____ _____ _____ _____
INACTIVE GAMES Word puzzles, chess, cards _____ _____ _____ _____	COLLECTIONS Stamps, coins, photos _____ _____ _____ _____	ENTERTAINMENT Books, eating out, shopping _____ _____ _____ _____
SPORTS & FITNESS Exercise, golf, skateboarding, cycling _____ _____ _____ _____	ARTS & MUSIC Writing, painting, music _____ _____ _____ _____	VOLUNTEERING Food bank, search and rescue _____ _____ _____ _____
TEAM SPORTS Softball, basketball, soccer _____ _____ _____ _____	CRAFTS Hand tools, sewing, models _____ _____ _____ _____	POLITICS Canvassing, petitions _____ _____ _____ _____
OUTDOOR ACTIVITIES Camping, bird watching _____ _____ _____ _____	TRAVEL Any kind _____ _____ _____ _____	SELF-IMPROVEMENT School or class _____ _____ _____ _____

Reprinted with permission from _Looking for Leisure in All the Right Places_ by Martin Kimeldorf.

Volunteer Interests Inventory

How would you like to explore your talents and interests while serving others? Check anything on this inventory that appeals strongly to you.

1. **Teach, counsel, coach, or care for others**

   ☐ tutor, teach, train, coach, mentor

   ☐ work with elderly, babies, children, disabled

   ☐ work with homeless, hungry, needy

   ☐ counsel individuals, peers, a support group

   ☐ assist in goodwill and cultural exchanges

   ☐ use hospitality or friendship skills as a guide or usher in museum, visitors' bureau, school, theater, club

   ☐ work in institutions or local agencies

   ☐ use leadership skills to organize a service project

   ☐ work with animals or pets

2. **Use my abilities with tools or equipment**

   ☐ preserve or conserve the environment

   ☐ repair or build things for others

   ☐ make or fix clothing or food

3. **Help with transportation or emergencies**

   ☐ distribute emergency or needed supplies—food, clothing, fuel, medical supplies

   ☐ transport people, items, or messages

   ☐ assist in local emergencies

4. **Use my artistic, athletic, or performing interests to benefit others**

   ☐ perform, announce, or help at benefits, sports events, art shows, museums, fairs, malls, etc.

   ☐ entertain people who are confined to home or nursing homes

   ☐ decorate or beautify areas, buildings, objects

   ☐ assist at local parks, recreation, and sports events

   ☐ create a video, audio tape, poster, display, or mural to help promote a cause or increase awareness

5. Use my business talents

☐ shop for others, advocate for consumers

☐ raise funds, collect donations or needed materials, work at auctions, work at concessions

☐ design an advertising campaign for a cause

☐ work on local business goals

☐ serve in a business organization

6. Use my office and communication skills

☐ help with typing, collating, mailing, filing, phoning, data entry

☐ use computers and related materials

☐ work on financial or record-keeping tasks

☐ use my writing skills

☐ work with libraries or archives

7. Use my scientific, health, or safety skills

☐ conduct surveys, studies, observations, research

☐ assist with health projects or programs

☐ increase public awareness about technology or science, health problems, safety issues

☐ use my math talents to help on projects

8. Participate in a youth, community, religious, or political organization

☐ join a cause, group, party, committee

☐ serve in a community service group, club, professional organization, religious group, foundation

☐ work on a project organized by a student club, class, committee, or living (residential) unit

☐ participate in an employee group, union, or professional organization

☐ join a long-term, stipended service such as VISTA, Peace Corps, Washington Service Corps

My Top Three Choices

Looking back over the items you checked, which three are the *most* interesting to you? Circle these three.

Reprinted with permission from *Community Service Learning Packet* by Martin Kimeldorf.

Vocabulary Words for Powerful Descriptions

1. Data Skills

accounted
administered
analyzed
analyzed statistics
articulated
audited
authored
budgeted
charted
classified
compared
computed
consolidated
coordinated
debated
designed
displayed

distributed
dramatized
edited
entered
evaluated
expressed
faxed
field tested
filed
financed
inventoried
investigated
logged
measured
organized
persuaded
polished

predicted
printed
promoted
published
queried
questioned
researched
responded
scheduled
sorted
studied
summarized
tabulated
telephoned
transmitted
typed

2. People Skills

accompanied
advised
assisted
cared for
coached
communicated
consulted
coordinated
counseled
demonstrated
directed
disciplined
elected
entertained
escorted

guided
hired
hosted
interviewed
inventoried
lectured
led
lobbied
managed
monitored
negotiated
networked
nursed
persuaded
piloted

pioneered
presented
promoted
protected
recruited
studied
supervised
supported
surveyed
tested
trained
transported
tutored
umpired
visited

3. Things Skills

adapted
arranged
assembled
assured quality
calibrated
cleansed
compared
composed
constructed
cooked
delivered
designed
enameled
experimented
explored
fabricated
fastened
forged

harvested
heat-treated
identified
illustrated
improved standards
inspected
installed
invented
inventoried
laminated
maintained
measured
minimized risk
modeled
operated
packaged
patented
performed

photographed
plotted
programmed
recorded
refined
regulated
renewed
repaired
rescued
set up
signaled
sized
sketched
tended
tested
tuned
welded

4. Character Traits, Temperaments, Work Habits, Self-Management Skills

Team Player
adaptable
broad- or open-minded
cooperative
democratic
fair-minded
flexible

Quality Oriented
accurate
careful
conscientious
deliberate
methodical
precise

Responsible Attitude
businesslike
mature
punctual
reliable
serious
steady
trustworthy

Positive Outlook
cheerful
enthusiastic
optimistic

Coping Skills
balanced values
copes with stress
good sense of humor
handles pressure

People Oriented
courteous
diplomatic
friendly
generous
good listener
good natured
helpful
kind
polite
sociable
tactful
warm

Thinking Traits
creative
curious
imaginative
innovative
inventive
logical
reflective
resourceful

Strong Work Ethic
competitive
efficient
energetic
hard-working
independent
industrious
motivated
persevering
persistent
quick
self-starter
tenacious
trainable

Personal Traits
adventurous
assertive
confident
courageous
gentle
healthy
idealistic
kind
loyal
neat
patient
practical
sensible
sensitive
well-groomed

Index

About
the Author

Martin Kimeldorf is the author of over 15 books and reports on the topics of job finding, leisure finding, community service, journal writing, and recreational drama. He holds Bachelor of Science degrees in technology education and liberal arts from Oregon State University and a Master's Degree in special education from Portland State University. He has taught in public schools, prisons, and colleges. He received the Literati Award from the *International Journal of Career Management* for Best Paper of the Year and has won other awards for teaching and playwriting. His hobbies include wood carving, painting, and magic. Martin lives with his wife, Judy, and their dog, Mitzi, in Tumwater, Washington.

Martin has created three portfolios and several scrapbooks on various topics. When looking for work in 1975, he used a teaching portfolio. When showing his paintings in 1993, he created an art portfolio. And when he began his studies of wood carving in the early 1970s, he created a personal portfolio with photos showing his work and the work of other people he admired.

Martin is also an experienced public speaker who has provided consultations and workshops for a wide variety of audiences. Topics include portfolio creation, résumé writing, job search training, community service, balancing work and leisure, and journal writing. To find out more about Martin's workshops, write to him c/o Free Spirit Publishing Inc., 400 First Avenue North, Suite 616, Minneapolis, MN 55401-1730.

MORE FREE SPIRIT BOOKS

The Kid's Guide to Service Projects:
Over 500 Service Ideas for Young
People Who Want to Make a Difference
by Barbara A. Lewis.
This guide has something for everyone who
wants to make a difference, from simple
projects to large-scale commitments. Kids
can choose from a variety of topics
including animals, crime fighting, the
environment, friendship, hunger, literacy,
politics and government, and transportation. A special section gives step-by-step
instructions for creating fliers, petitions,
press releases, and more.
$10.95, 192 pp., s/c, 6" x 9".

Respecting Our Differences:
A Guide to Getting Along in a
Changing World
by Lynn Duvall
Learn about the issues involved in preju-
dice and discrimination; find out how
and why to become more tolerant of
others. Includes real-life examples of
teenagers from across the United States
who are working to promote tolerance.
$12.95; 208 pp.; illus.; B&W photos;
s/c; 6" x 9".

School Power:
Strategies for Succeeding in School
*by Jeanne Shay Schumm, Ph.D.,
and Marguerite Radencich, Ph.D.*
The most comprehensive study skills handbook available. Covers getting organized,
taking notes, studying smarter, writing
better, following directions, handling
homework, managing long-term assignments, and more.
$13.95; 132 pp.; illus.; B&W photos;
s/c; 8 ½" x 11"

Bringing Up Parents:
The Teenager's Handbook
by Alex J. Packer, Ph.D.
Straight talk and specific suggestions on
how you can take the initiative to resolve
conflicts with your parents, improve
family relationships, earn trust, accept
responsibility, and help create a healthier,
happier home environment.
$14.95; 272 pp.; illus.; s/c; 7 ¼" x 9 ¼"

A Gebra Named Al
by Wendy Isdell
Julie falls asleep while doing her
algebra and wakes up in a strange land
where she meets a gebra named Al. Join
Julie and Al on their journey through the
Land of Mathematics, where the Orders
of Operations are real places, and fruits
that look like Bohr models grow on
chemistrees.
$4.95; 136 pp.; s/c; 5 ½" x 7 ½"

The Kid's Guide to Social Action:
How to Solve the Social Problems
You Choose—and Turn Creative
Thinking into Positive Action
(Revised, Updated, and Expanded)
by Barbara A. Lewis
A comprehensive guide to making a difference in the world. Includes tips on letter-
writing, interviewing, speechmaking,
fundraising, lobbying Congress, getting
media coverage, and more.
$14.95; 208 pp.; illus.; B&W photos;
s/c; 8 ½" x 11"

The First Honest Book About Lies
by Jonni Kincher
Discusses the nature of lies and how we
live with them every day—at home, at
school, in our relationships, and in our
culture. You'll learn how to search for
truth; become an active, intelligent ques-
tioner; and explore your own feelings
about lies.
$12.95; 200 pp.; illus.; s/c; 8" x 10"

Can You Find It?
25 Library Scavenger Hunts
to Sharpen Your Research Skills
by Randall McCutcheon
An unorthodox tour of the library,
guided by cartoons, quotes, and cryptic
clues. You'll learn why Whoopi Goldberg
worked at a mortuary, the origin of the
expression "running amok," and other
fascinating facts found in dictionaries,
directories, indexes, encyclopedias, and
other sources.
$10.95; 208 pp.; illus.; s/c; 5 ½" x 8 ½"

Find these books in your favorite bookstore, or contact:

Free Spirit Publishing Inc.
400 First Avenue North • Suite 616 • Minneapolis, MN 55401-1724
toll-free (800) 735-7323 • local (612) 338-2068 • fax (612) 337-5050
www.freespirit.com• help4kids@freespirit.com